JUL - - 2015

If you were me and lived in...
PERU

A Child's Introduction to Cultures Around the World

Carole P. Roman

Dedicated to my assistant, Christina.

I am so happy to have you working with me!

ISBN: 1499640692

ISBN 13: 9781499640694

Library of Congress Control Number: 2014909566

CreateSpace Independent Publishing Platform

North Charleston, South Carolina

If you were me and lived in Peru (Pir-roo), you would find your home in the western part of South America on the coast of the Pacific Ocean. The country is called the Republic of Peru. It has many different climates. You can go from the dry plains to the wet Amazon (Am-a-zon) Rain Forest and to a high mountain range called the Andes (Ann-dees). Peru is home to some of the world's oldest civilizations. People have lived there for over ten thousand years.

You might live in Lima (Lee-ma), which is the capital of Peru. It is a large city overlooking the ocean with a population of nine million people. One third of the Peruvian (Per-roo-vee-an) population lives there. The word Lima comes from an old Indian word, limaq (li-mack), which means "talker."

Your parents might have named you Hugo (Hew-go), Fernando (Fer-nan-doh), or Gerardo (Ger-ar-doh) if you are a boy. Sometimes they pick Rosario (Ro-sar-e-o), Carmen (Car-men), or Teresa (Ter-ray-her) if you are a girl.

You would call your mommy, Mami (Mammee). When you see your daddy, you would call him Papi (Pap-pee).

Nuevos soles (new-way-vos sol-les) is the type of money you would use to buy a muñeca (moon-yek-a) for your little sister. Can you guess what that is?

When visitors come, you could take them to Machu Picchu (Mat-chu Pik-chu). It is a beautiful and ancient city built high up on a mountain by the Incas (Ink-as) in about the year 1450. Its name means "old peak" or "old mountaintop." The Incas used the sides of the mountains as farmland and made terraces to grow their food. Terraces are strips of land cut into the sides of the mountain so they could farm the rocky soil.

If you want to eat afterward, Peru has many different types of food. In Lima you would eat seafood and get ceviche (ci-vee-che), which is raw white fish that is soaked in lemon or lime, onion, and chilies, and then cut into bite-size pieces. You might prefer cuy (koo-ee), which is fried guinea pig. In the old days, it was only eaten by Incan kings. Maybe you'd choose papa rellena (pa-pa re-yen-ah), a mashed potato stuffed with ground meat and spices. Since potatoes come from Peru, you would eat a lot of them. They say there are four thousand kinds of potatoes. Your favorite way to finish the meal might be picarones (pik-ha-row-nes), fried doughnuts served with syrup.

You would love to play the game sapito (sa-peet-o) with your friends. You would place a palm-size toy frog in the center of many boxes and try to throw a coin into its mouth. Whoever got the most coins in the frog would win.

In Peru, boys enjoy playing fútbol, while girls have fun playing volleyball. Which game would you like to play?

Every year in February you would celebrate Carnival (Car-na-val). During the festival, everybody has squirt guns, water balloons, and buckets of water.

You would roam the streets and surprise other people by ambushing them and getting them soaking wet. You would be very wet, too, because they would do the same to you!

When you go to colegio (co-le-hee-o), you would tell everybody about how many people you soaked.

So you see, if you were me, how life in Peru could really be.

Pronunciation Guide

Amazon Rain Forest (Am-a-zon)- a thick, lush rain forest that is found in South America.

Andes (Ann-dees)- high mountain range in Peru.

Carmen (Car-men)- popular girl's name.

Carnival (Car-na-val)- popular holiday filled with great food and games.

cerviche (ci-vee-che)- little pieces of raw fish cut up and soaked in lemon or lime.

colegio (col-le-hee-o)- school.

cuy (koo-ee)- fried guinea pig.

Fernando (Fer-nan-doh)- popular boy's name.

fútbol (fut-bol)- soccer.

Gerardo (Ger-ar-doh)- popular boy's name.

Hugo (Hew-go)- popular boy's name.

Incas (Ink-as)- ancient people of Peru.

Lima (Lee-ma)- capital of Peru.

Limaq (li-mack)- Indian word that means "talker."

Machu Picchu (Mat-chu Pik-chu)- ancient city built high up on a mountaintop, by the Incas. Its name means "old peak."

Mami (Mam-mee)- Mommy.

muñeca (moon-yek-a)- doll.

nuevos soles (new-vay-os sol-les)- money of Peru.

papa rellena (pa-pa re-yen-ah)- mashed potato stuffed with ground meat and spices.

Papi (Pap-pee)- Daddy.

Peru (Pir-roo)- country in the western part of South America.

Peruvian (Per-roo-ve-an)- the people of Peru.

picarones (pik-ha-row-nes)- fried doughnuts.

Rosario (Ro-sar-e-o)- popular girl's name.

sapito (sa-peet-to)- popular game in Peru that children play.

Teresa (Ter-ray-her)- popular girl's name.

Made in the USA
Charleston, SC
11 May 2015